Anatomy And Physiology For Kids

Speedy Publishing LLC
40 E. Main St. #1156
Newark, DE 19711

www.speedypublishing.com

Copyright 2014
9781681275512
First Printed January 7, 2015

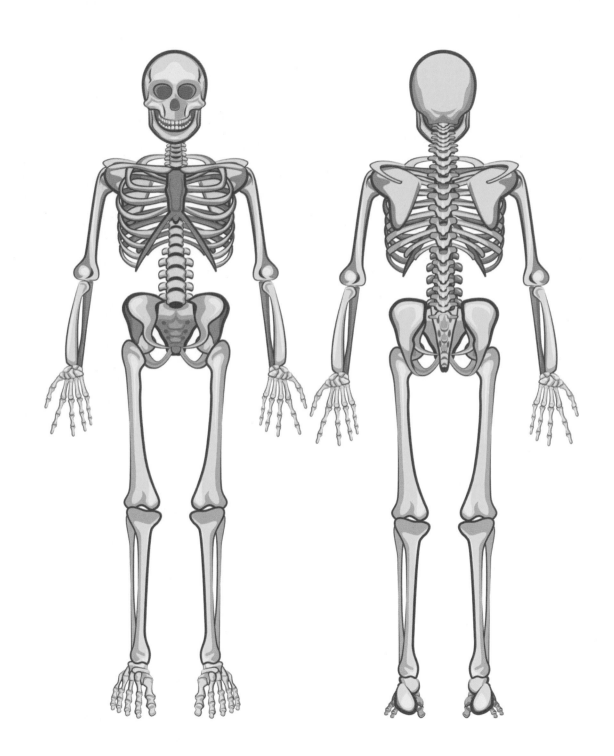

Did you know?

The skeletal system includes all of the bones and joints in the body. Each bone is a complex living organ that is made up of many cells, protein fibers, and minerals. The skeleton acts as a scaffold by providing support and protection for the soft tissues that make up the rest of the body. The skeletal system also provides attachment points for muscles to allow movements at the joints. New blood cells are produced by the red bone marrow inside of our bones.

Did you know?

The muscular system is responsible for the movement of the human body. Attached to the bones of the skeletal system are about 700 named muscles that make up roughly half of a person's body weight. Each of these muscles is a discrete organ constructed of skeletal muscle tissue, blood vessels, tendons, and nerves. Muscle tissue is also found inside of the heart, digestive organs, and blood vessels.

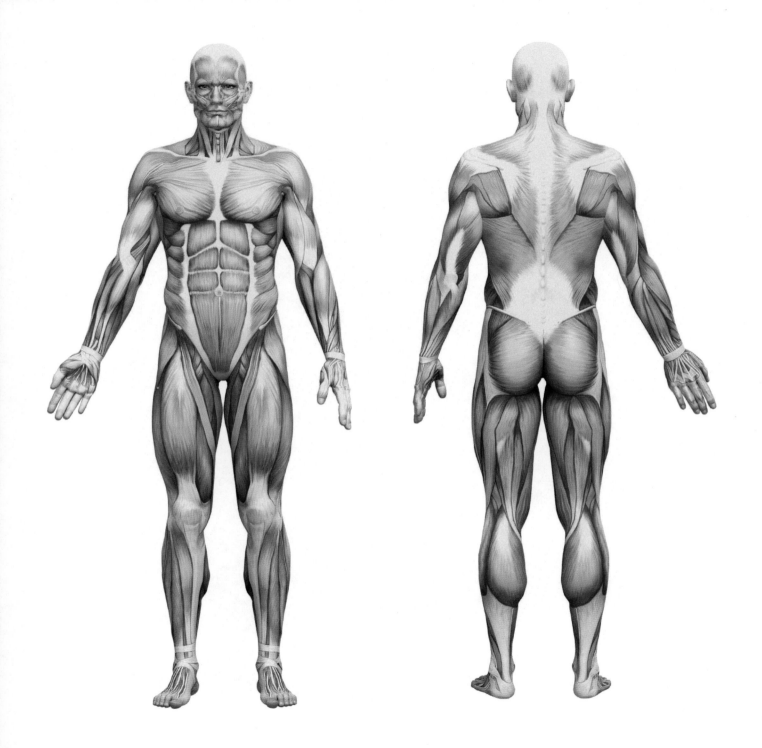

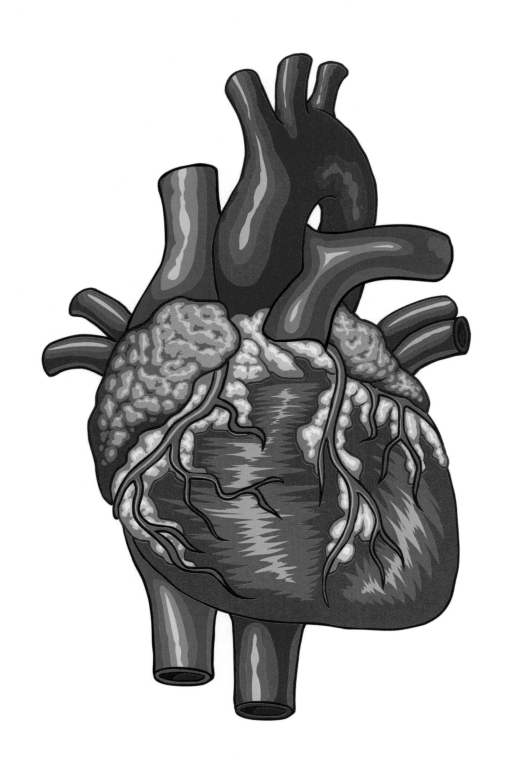

Did you know?

The heart is one of the most important organs in the human body, continuously pumping blood around our body through blood vessels. Your heart is located in your chest and is well protected by your rib cage. Electricity going through your heart makes the muscle cells contract.

Did you know?

The human brain is like a powerful computer that stores our memory and controls how we as humans think and react. It has evolved over time and features some incredibly intricate parts that scientists still struggle to understand. The brain contains billions of nerve cells that send and receive information around the body.

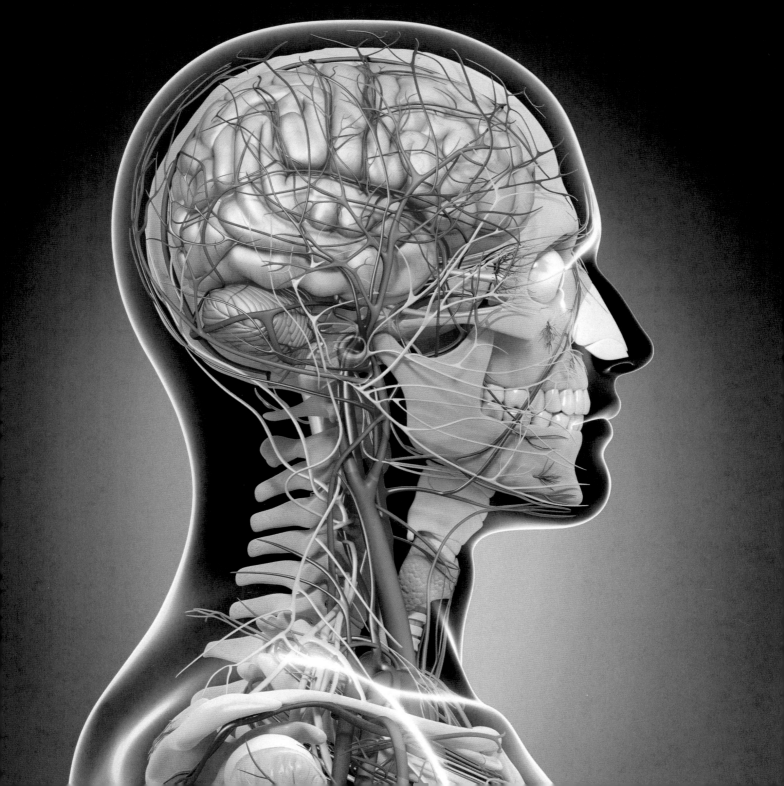

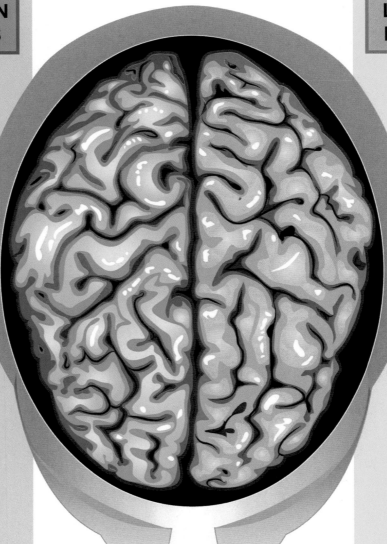

RIGHT-BRAIN FUNCTIONS

Art awareness

Creativity

Imagination

Intuition

Insight

Holistic thought

Music awareness

3-D forms

Left-hand control

LEFT-BRAIN FUNCTIONS

Analytic thought

Logic

Language

Reasoning

Science and math

Written

Numbers skills

Right-hand control

Did you know?

Each side of the brain interacts largely with just one half of the body, but for reasons that are not yet fully understood, the interaction is with opposite sides, the right side of the brain interacts with the left side of the body, and vice versa. The brain is the center of the human nervous system, controlling our thoughts, movements, memories and decisions.

Did you know?

Skin is the human body's largest organ (an organ is a group of tissues that work together to perform functions in your body, others include your brain, heart and lungs). Your skin performs a range of different functions which include physically protecting your bones, muscles and internal organs, protecting your body from outside diseases, allowing you to feel and react to heat and cold and using blood to regulate your body heat.

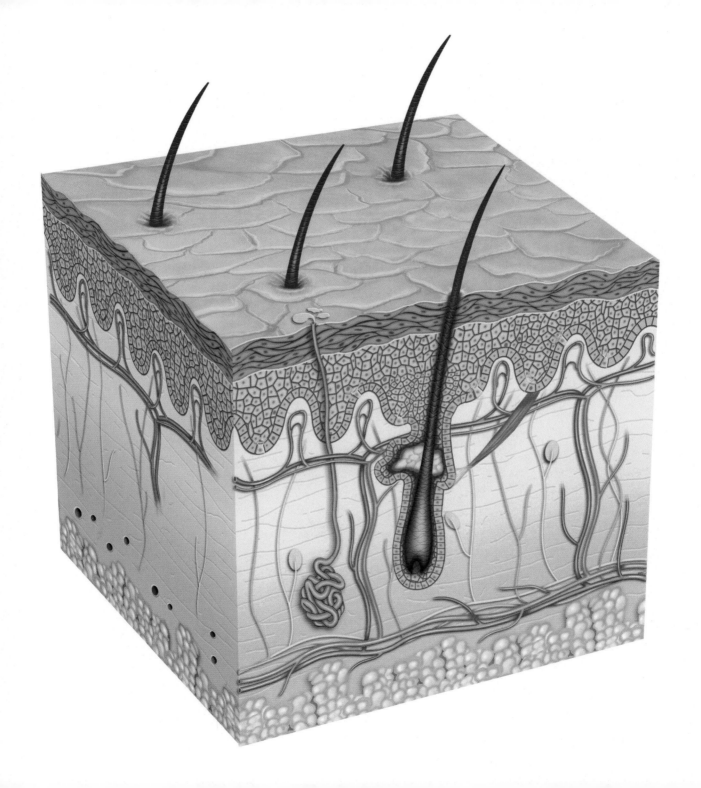

Erythrocytes

Did you know?

Red blood cells have the important job of carrying oxygen around the body. They also contain a protein called hemoglobin. Hemoglobin contains iron which combines with oxygen to give hemoglobin and our blood, a red color. Blood makes up around 7% of the weight of a human body.

Did you know?

Capillaries are tiny, averaging about 8 microns (1/3000 inch) in diameter, or about a tenth of the diameter of a human hair. Red blood cells are about the same size as the capillaries through which they travel, so these cells must move in single-file lines.

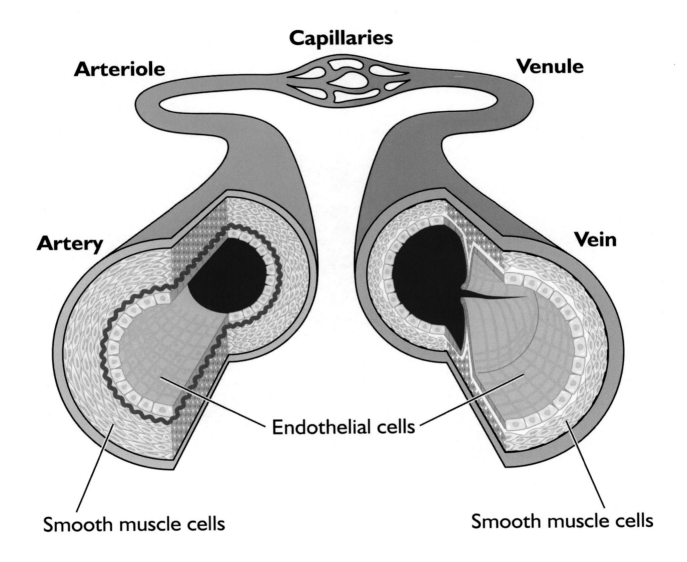

Capillaries

Arteriole

Venule

Artery

Vein

Endothelial cells

Smooth muscle cells

Smooth muscle cells

Human Eye Anatomy

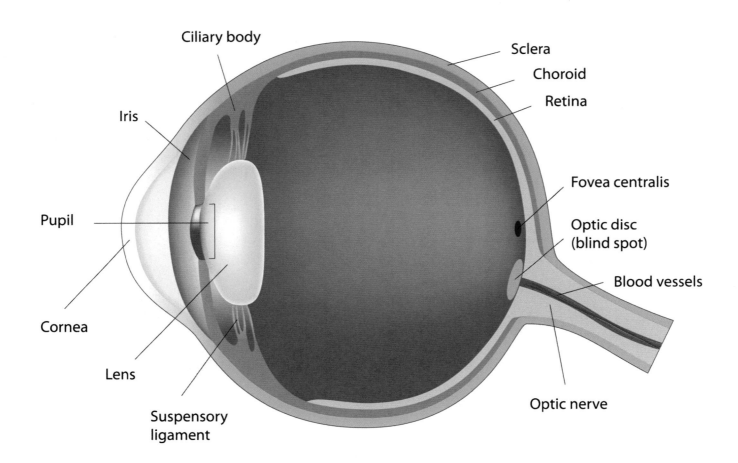

Ciliary body

Sclera

Choroid

Retina

Iris

Pupil

Fovea centralis

Optic disc
(blind spot)

Blood vessels

Cornea

Lens

Suspensory
ligament

Optic nerve

Did you know?

The information our eyes receive is sent to our brain along the optic nerve. This information is then processed by our brain and helps us make appropriate decisions, for example if you can see an object flying in your direction then you will probably move quickly out of the way.

Did you know?

Teeth are used to help break down food. Humans form 2 sets of teeth over the course of their lives. Baby teeth are usually replaced by adult teeth between the ages of 6 and 12. Teeth are covered in a hard substance called enamel.

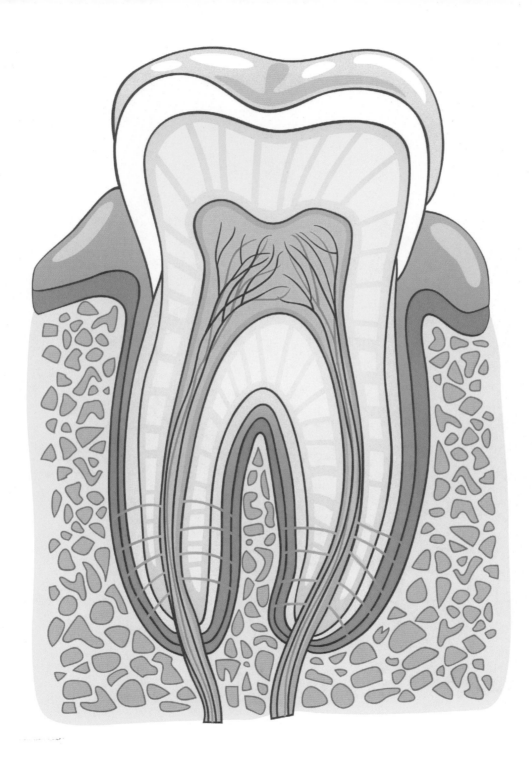

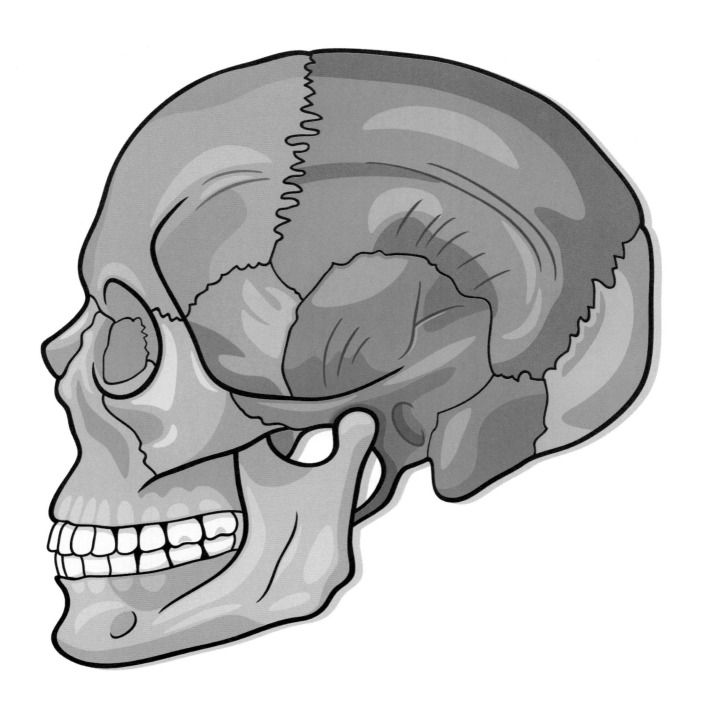

Did you know?

The skull or cranium is the hard, bone case that contains and protects your brain. The skull looks as though it is a single bone. In fact, it is made up of 22 separate bones, cemented together along rigid joints called sutures.

Did you know?

The nose has special cells which help us smell. Your nose can help detect dangerous chemicals in the air. The human nose can smell many different odors but is far less sensitive than other animals such as dogs.

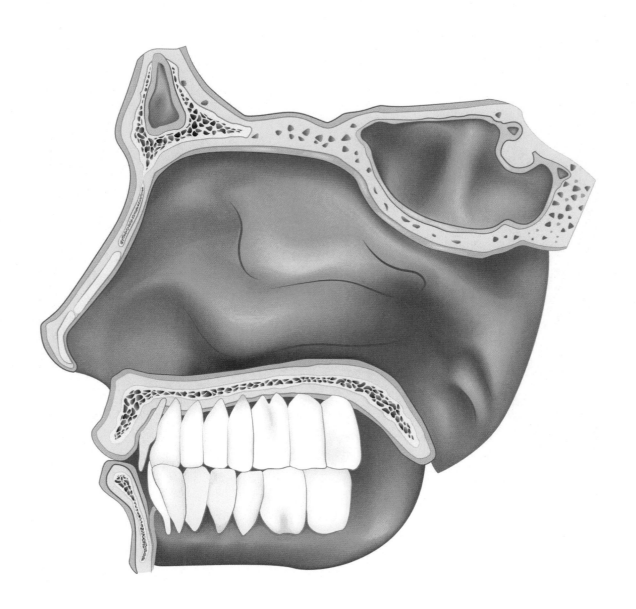

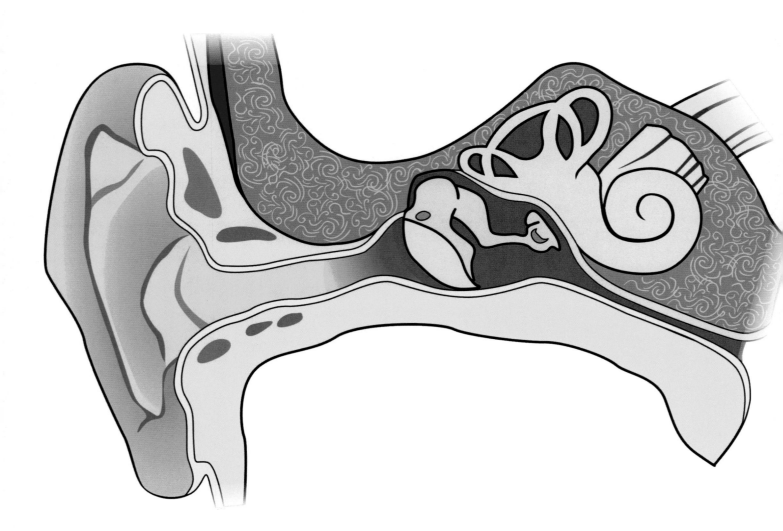

Did you know?

Our ears help us detect sound. Ears convert sound waves into nerve impulses that are sent to the brain. While your ears pick up the sound, it is your brain that does the hard work of making sense of it all.

Did you know?

The liver carries out over 200 different functions in the body, which include providing glucose for the brain, filtering toxins that may enter your body, battles infection, and stores nutrients and vitamins.

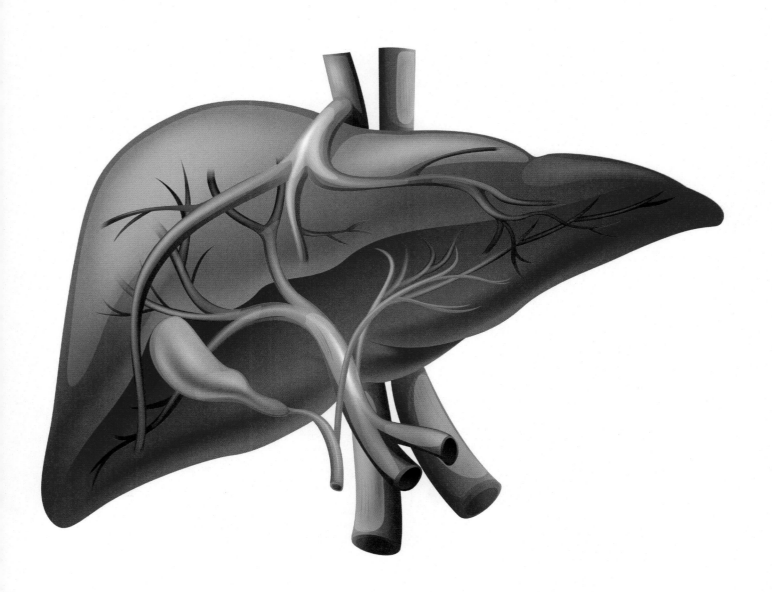

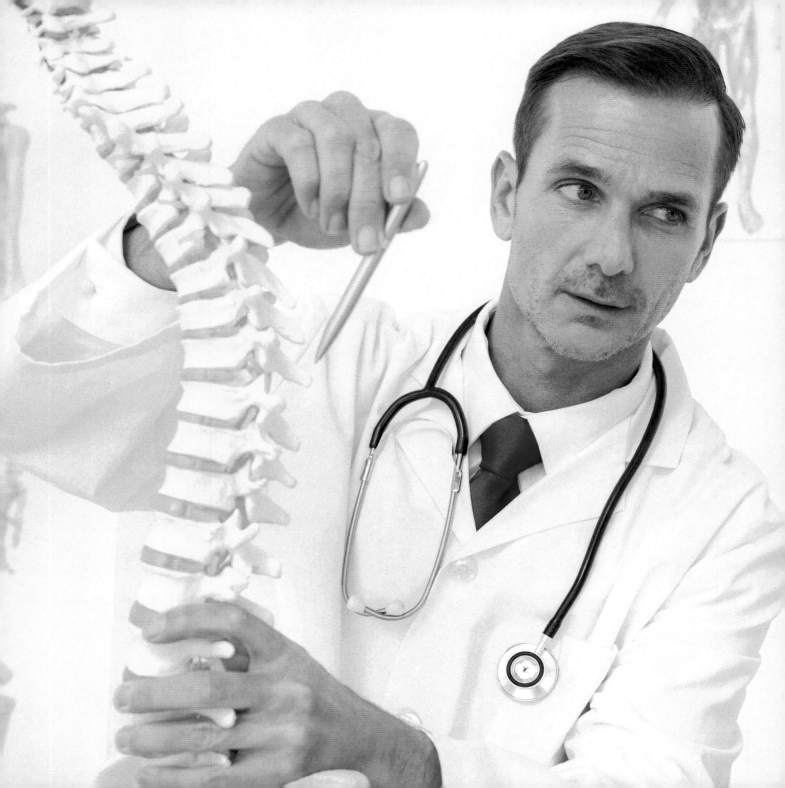

Did you know?

The spinal column or backbone is instrumental to the strength, support, flexibility and range of movement our bodies possess. It's a complicated structure, with many interconnected and interdependent components.

Did you know?

Each human has two kidneys, one on the right side, and one on the left side, in the middle of the back, which are both protected by the rib cage. The kidneys filter all of the waste products from your blood and pass them into the urine. Your kidneys are also responsible for keeping things in your blood balanced - acid, electrolytes such as sodium and potassium, sugars, and proteins.

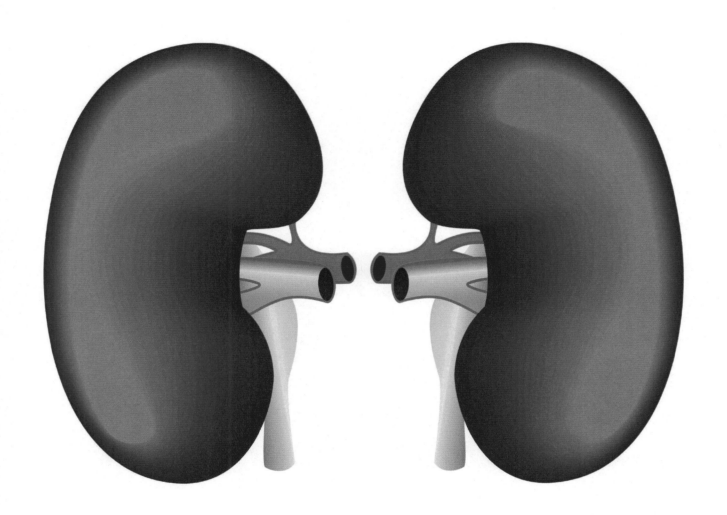

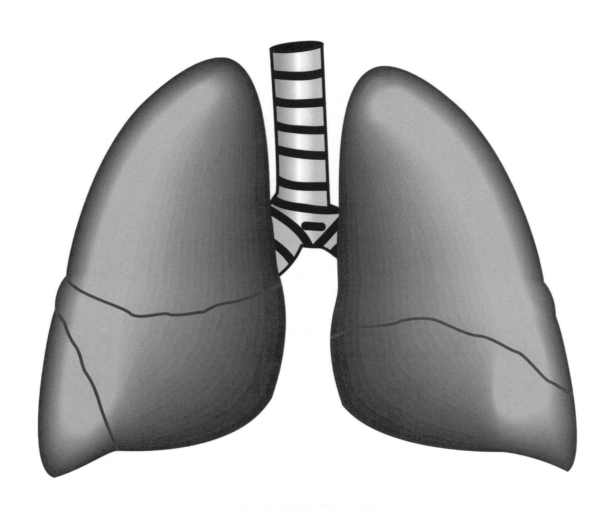

Did you know?

The primary functions of your lungs are to transport oxygen from the air you breathe into your bloodstream while taking away carbon dioxide, which is released into the air when you breathe out. Your left and right lungs aren't exactly the same. The lung on the left side of your body is divided into two lobes while the lung on your right side is divided into three. The left lung is also slightly smaller, allowing room for your heart.

Did you know?

The mouth allows us to talk, to smile or frown, and to whistle. The mouth, working with the teeth and tongue, allow us to have speech, and also allows us to eat our food. Our teeth allow us to chew up our food so our body can swallow and digest it easier, and are among the hardest substances in the body.

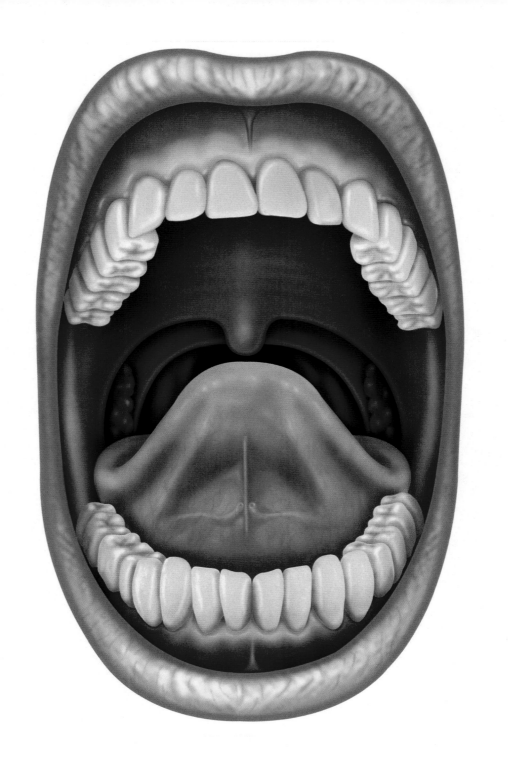

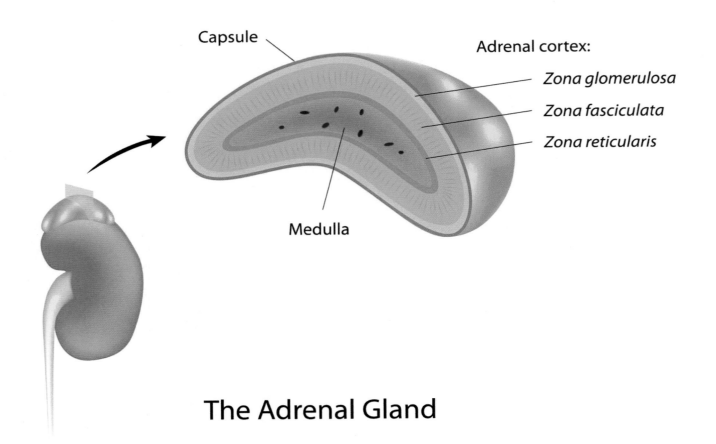

Capsule

Adrenal cortex:

Zona glomerulosa

Zona fasciculata

Zona reticularis

Medulla

The Adrenal Gland

Did you know?

The adrenal glands (also known as suprarenal glands) are endocrine glands that are located on the top of the kidneys. They are chiefly responsible for releasing hormones in response to stress through the synthesis of corticosteroids such as cortisol and catecholamines such as adrenaline (epinephrine) and noradrenaline.

Did you know?

The pancreas has two general jobs which are very important. It releases digestive juices (enzymes) and that process is called an exocrine function. The other general job it does is putting different chemical messengers called hormones into your blood, which help with a wide variety of functions in your body. This job is called an endocrine process.

PANCREAS

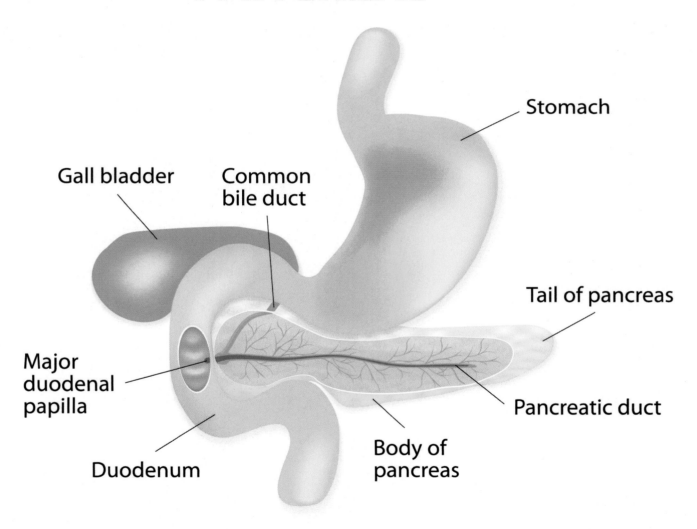

Stomach

Gall bladder

Common bile duct

Tail of pancreas

Major duodenal papilla

Pancreatic duct

Duodenum

Body of pancreas

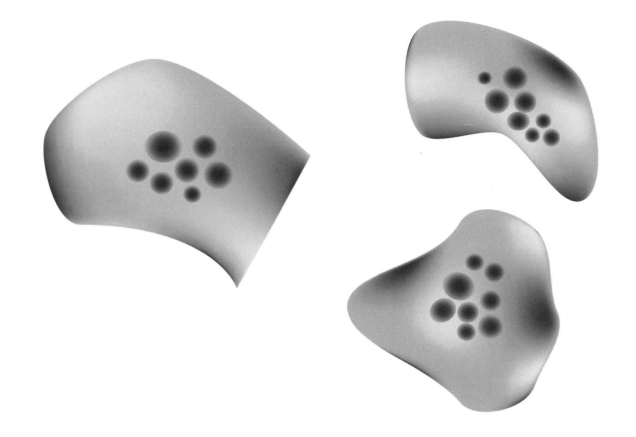

Platelets

Did you know?

Platelets (thrombocytes) are colorless blood cells that play an important role in blood clotting. Platelets stop blood loss by clumping and forming plugs in blood vessel holes.

Did you know?

Your stomach, which is attached to your mouth by a long tube called the esophagus, is the first place your food starts to get broken down into molecules your body can use, which is a process called digestion.

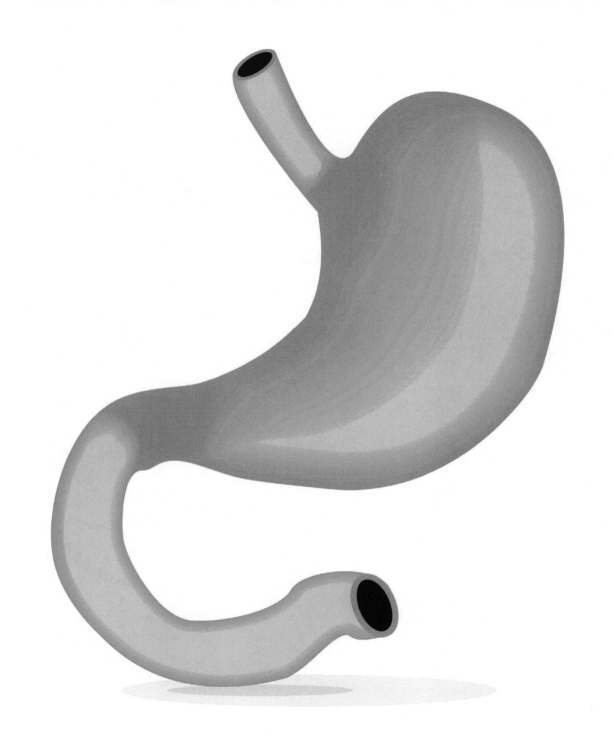

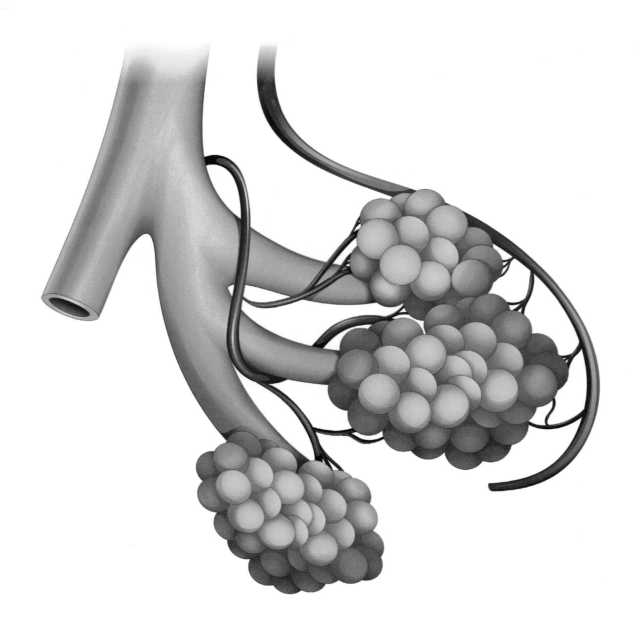

Did you know?

These alveoli are located at the ends of the air passageways in the lungs. They have very thin (one cell thick), wet walls and are surrounded with a network of small blood vessels, or capillaries. This allows gases to diffuse, or move across, the surface of the alveolus. Inside the alveoli is where a gas exchange occurs.

Made in the USA
Las Vegas, NV
19 September 2021